D0787262

Renzo Piano

Renzo Piano

teNeues

Editor in chief:
Paco Asensio

Editor and original texts:
Aurora Cuito

English translation:
Mathew Clarke

German translation:
Inken Wolthaus

French translation:
Michel Ficerai

Italian translation:
Grazia Suffriti

Art direction:
Mireia Casanovas Soley

Graphic Design / Layout:
Emma Termes Parera and Soti Mas-Bagà

Published worldwide by teNeues Publishing Group
(except Spain, Portugal and South-America):

teNeues Book Division
Neuer Zollhof 1, 40221 Düsseldorf, Germany
Tel: 0049-(0)211-994597-0
Fax: 0049-(0)211-994597-40

teNeues Publishing Company
16 West 22nd Street, New York, N.Y., 10010, USA
Tel.: 001-212-627-9090
Fax: 001-212-627-9511

teNeues Publishing UK Ltd.
Aldwych House, 71/91 Aldwych
London WC2B 4HN, UK
Tel.: 0044-1892-837-171
Fax: 0044-1892-837-272

teNeues France S.A.R.L.
140, rue de la Croix Nivert
75015 Paris, France
Tel.: 0033-1-5576-6205
Fax: 0033-1-5576-6419

www.teneues.com

Editorial project:

© 2002 **LOFT** Publications
Domènech 7-9, 2° 2ª
08012 Barcelona, Spain
Tel.: 0034 932 183 099
Fax: 0034 932 370 060
e-mail: loft@loftpublications.com
www.loftpublications.com

Printed by:
Gráficas Anman. Sabadell, Spain.

September 2002

ISBN: 3-8238-5584-0

We would like to show sincere gratefulness to the Renzo Piano
Building Workshop, specially Giovanna Giusto and Stefania Canta for
their useful collaboration.

This book presents the ten most representative projects undertaken in the last few years by the firm that Piano runs from Genoa, Paris and Berlin. Its name, Renzo Piano Building Workshop, indicates the construction tradition that he inherited from his family, which has led him to be faithful to his materials, by pushing them to their limits, improving their performance and enhancing their characteristics.

Furthermore, Renzo Piano's work is based on a search for the human face of technology, on an attempt to demonstrate that modern building processes do not inevitably lead to cold, mechanized industrial buildings, but can give rise to warm, luminous spaces catering to the needs of human beings. Piano brings the spirit of the small-scale craftsman to large infrastructures, painstakingly perfecting the details of a precious object. Technology is used in all his projects to tone down light, evaluate the context and find a means to integrate them into nature. After designing buildings where technology represented an end in itself, Piano moved towards projects in which innovative building techniques are merely a tool used to obtain comfortable, sustainable and ecological spaces.

Dieser Band zeigt die repräsentativen Projekte der letzten Jahre, die Piano von Genua, Paris und Berlin aus leitete. Der Name, Renzo Piano Building Workshop, spricht für die konstruktive Tradition, die der Architekt von seiner Familie erbte, und die ihn lehrte, den Materialien treu zu bleiben, deren Grenzen zu erforschen, die Ergebnisse zu verbessern und die Eigenschaften zu potenzieren.

Das Werk Renzo Pianos basiert andererseits auf der Suche nach der menschlichen Seite der Technologie, darauf zu prüfen und zu beweisen, dass die Modernisierung der konstruktiven Verfahren keine kalten, mechanisierten und industriellen Gebäude zur Folge haben muss, sondern dass dadurch lichtvolle und warmtönige Räume nach Maß und den Bedürfnissen des Menschen entsprechend geschaffen werden können. Für die großen Infrastrukturen holt Piano den Geist des kleinen Handwerkers wieder hervor, der die Details eines kostbaren Gegenstandes liebevoll verbessert. Bei allen seinen Projekten dient die Technologie dazu, das Licht zu beleben, das Umfeld zu respektieren und die Integration in die Natur zu ermöglichen, anstatt Gebäude zu planen, bei denen die Technologie Methode und Ziel bedeutet. Der Architekt aus Genua fällt durch Werke auf, bei denen die innovativen konstruktiven Techniken lediglich das Werkzeug sind, um komfortable, solide und ökologische Räume zu gestalten.

Ce volume présente les dix projets les plus représentatifs des dernières années, menés par l'étude dirigée par Piano depuis Gênes, Paris et Berlin. Son nom, le Renzo Piano Building Workshop, indique la tradition de construction héritée par l'architecte de sa famille. Elle l'a conduit à être plus fidèle aux matériaux, à en explorer les limites, à améliorer leur rendement et à en renforcer les propriétés.

D'un autre côté, l'œuvre de Renzo Piano repose sur la recherche de l'aspect humain de la technologie, en utilisant, essayant et démontrant que la modernisation des procédés de construction ne doit pas nécessairement engendrer des bâtiments froids, mécanisés et industriels. Bien au contraire, elle peut donner naissance à des espaces lumineux et chaleureux, aux dimensions de l'homme et répondant à ses attentes. Piano récupère pour les grandes infrastructures l'esprit du petit artisan qui offre une réponse soigneuse à chaque détail d'un objet précieux. Dans tous ses projets, la technologie est destinée à nuancer la lumière, à valoriser le contexte et rendre possible l'intégration dans la nature. Après avoir conçu des édifices où la technologie était à la fois méthode et fin, l'architecte génois évolue vers des œuvres pour lesquelles les techniques de construction novatrices sont uniquement un outil permettant d'obtenir des espaces confortables, viables et écologiques.

Questo volume presenta i dieci progetti più rappresentativi realizzati negli ultimi anni dallo studio che Piano dirige da Genova, Parigi e Berlino. Il suo nome, Renzo Piano Building Workshop, indica la tradizione costruttiva che l'architetto ha ereditato dalla sua famiglia, che l'ha portato ad essere fedele ai materiali, ad esplorare i loro limiti, a migliorare la loro resa, ed a potenziare le loro proprietà.

L'opera di Renzo Piano, d'altra parte, è basata sulla ricerca del lato umano della tecnologia, nell'utilizzare, provare e dimostrare che la modernizzazione dei processi costruttivi non deve necessariamente generare edifici freddi, meccanizzati e industriali, ma che può dar origine a spazi che rispettino la misura e le necessità dell'uomo, luminosi ed accoglienti. Piano recupera per le grandi infrastrutture lo spirito del piccolo artigiano che risolve con attenzione i dettagli di un oggetto pregiato. In tutti i suoi progetti la tecnologia è destinata a sottolineare la luce, a dar valore al contesto ed a rendere possibile l'integrazione con la natura. Dopo aver progettato edifici dove la tecnologia costituiva il metodo ed il fine, l'architetto genovese simpatizza ora per opere dove le tecniche costruttive innovatrici sono solo strumenti per ottenere spazi confortevoli, sostenibili ed ecologici.

Columbus International Exhibition

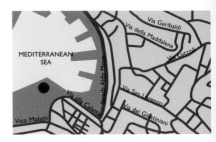

Location: Porto Antico, Genoa, Italy
Date of construction: 1985–1992
Photographers: Shunji Ishida, Publifoto, Banchero, Michel Denancé, Emanuela Minetti

In the late 1980s Genoa's local authorities decided to organize an international exhibition to mark the fifth centenary of the discovery of America. The land chosen for the event formed part of the city's old port, and so the project also had the opportunity – and duty – to regenerate the area. The project had to create a connection between the historic center and the sea, which until then had been separated by old warehouses, a railroad track and a freeway. The development included the conversion of the old buildings once used to store cotton into public spaces, such as a library and an auditorium. Although new buildings were also erected – an aquarium, for example – the design process always took great care not to alter the original spirit of the area.The port and the city were connected by extending the small alleyways leading from the historic center down to the sea; the Via del Mare, for example, ended up going right into the heart of the port, which is now thronged with both locals and tourists alike, strolling and enjoying the activities taking place by the waterside.

À la fin des années 80 du XXème siècle, l'administration génoise décida d'organiser une exposition internationale afin de célébrer le cinquième centenaire de la découverte des Amériques. Le terrain choisi pour accueillir l'événement fait partie de l'ancien port de la ville, le projet ayant par conséquent également la possibilité et le devoir de régénérer la zone. L'intervention devait créer une connexion entre le centre historique et la mer, jusqu'alors séparés par d'anciens locaux industriels, une voie ferrée et une autoroute. Le développement inclut la reconversion des anciens entrepôts, où était conservé le coton, en espaces publics, ainsi une bibliothèque ou un auditorium. Bien que de nouvelles constructions aient pu voir le jour, un aquarium notamment, le processus de création porta une attention toute spéciale au respect de l'esprit originel de la zone. La con-nexion entre le port et la ville naquit de l'extension de petites ruelles du centre historique jusqu'à la mer, ainsi la Via del Mare qui mène aujourd'hui au cœur de la zone portuaire, et dont les allées sont à présent bondées de génois et de touristes à même de profiter des activités au bord de l'eau.

Gegen Ende der achtziger Jahre des 20. Jahrhunderts beschloss die Stadtverwaltung von Genua in Erinnerung an die Entdeckung Amerikas vor fünfhundert Jahren eine internationale Ausstellung zu organisieren. Der für dieses Ereignis vorgesehene Platz liegt im alten Hafen der Stadt, wodurch das Projekt die Chance und zugleich die Verpflichtung hatte, zur Verbesserung dieser Gegend beizutragen. Es sollte eine Verbindung zwischen dem historischen Stadtzentrum und dem Meer geschaffen werden, die bis dahin durch alte Lagerhäuser, Bahngleise und eine Autobahn voneinander getrennt waren. Das Projekt umfasste den Umbau alter Hallen, in denen bisher Baumwolle gelagert wurde, in beispielsweise eine Bibliothek und einen Konzertsaal. Obwohl auch neue Gebäude erbaut wurden, z. B. ein Aquarium, war man immer bemüht, den ursprünglichen Charakter dieser Gegend nicht zu verändern. Für die Verbindung zwischen Hafen und Stadt verlängerte man die engen Gassen des historischen Stadtzentrums bis hin zum Meer. Hier ist die Via del Mare zu erwähnen, die heute bis in das Herz des Hafens führt und auf der sich jetzt Genuesen und Touristen drängen und am Wasser ihren Aktivitäten nachgehen.

Alla fine degli anni '80 del XX° secolo l'amministrazione genovese decise di organizzare un'esposizione per celebrare il V° centenario della scoperta dell'America. Il terreno scelto per la celebrazione dell'evento forma parte dell'antico porto della città, per cui il progetto aveva anche l'opportunità di riqualificare la zona. L'intervento doveva creare un collegamento tra il centro storico ed il mare, che fino ad allora erano stati separati a causa della presenza di vecchi magazzini, dei binari della ferrovia e di un'autostrada. La progettazione ha inserito la riconversione degli antichi capannoni dove si conservava il cotone in spazi pubblici, come ad esempio una biblioteca ed un auditorio. Anche se sono stati costruiti nuovi edifici, come un acquario, il processo di progettazione è stato retto da una particolare attenzione nel non alterare lo spirito originario della zona. Il collegamento tra il porto e la città è stato realizzato mediante il prolungamento delle piccole strade del centro storico fino al mare, come la Via del Mare che attualmente porta fino al cuore del porto, i cui lungomare sono pieni ora di genovesi e turisti che approfittano delle attività vicine all'acqua.

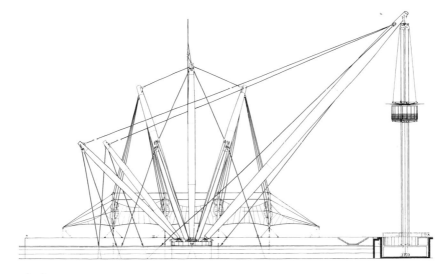

Section
Schnitt
Section
Sezione

0 2 4

Beyeler Foundation

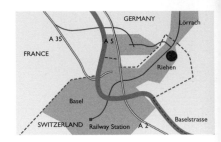

Location: Baselstrasse 77, Riehen, Basel, Switzerland
Date of construction: 1991–1997
Photographers: Michel Denancé, Christian Richters, Niggi Brauning

The art collector Ernst Beyeler commissioned Renzo Piano's firm to build a museum to house his collection. The client gave a concise brief as he had a very clear idea of what the building should be like. Firstly, the museum had to be integrated into the surrounding landscape – the park, originally private, that encircles the magnificent Villa Berower, a historic monument in Switzerland's Riehen district; secondly, the galleries had to be lit by overhead natural lighting. Starting from these two premises, the project consisted of four supporting walls, equal in length and set in parallel to the wall surrounding the site. All the walls were covered with sandstone from Argentina, similar to the local stone but more resistant to bad weather. The whole structure is topped with a slightly sloping glass roof, which looks as if it is floating on top of the building, as its light metal structure is virtually imperceptible from the inside. Some of the façades are made of glass, so the relationship between the interior and exterior is very intense, and the galleries benefit from the peace that reigns over the whole site.

L'amateur d'art Ernst Beyeler commanda à l'étude de Renzo Piano la construction d'un musée pour héberger sa collection. Les impératifs du client, qui avait une vision très claire de la nature de l'œuvre, se sont avérés concis. D'un côté, le musée devait se fondre dans le paysage environnant, le parc jadis privé qui entoure la magnifique Villa Berower, un monument historique de la ville suisse de Riehen. D'un autre côté, les salles devaient être baignées de lumière zénithale. Partant de ces deux prémisses, le projet repose sur quatre murs de charge d'égales longueurs et disposés parallèlement à la paroi fermant le terrain. Chacun fut revêtu de grès d'Argentine, qui n'est pas sans rappeler la pierre locale tout en offrant une meilleure résistance aux rigueurs du temps. L'ensemble est couvert par un toit de verre légèrement incliné qui semble flotter au-dessus de l'édifice grâce à une structure métallique légère et quasi imperceptible depuis l'intérieur. Certaines façades sont vitrées, la relation intérieur-extérieur se révélant ainsi intense et les salles bénéficient du calme emplissant le lieu.

Der Kunstsammler Ernst Beyeler beauftragte das Studio Renzo Piano mit dem Bau eines Museums für seine Kollektion. Die Anforderungen des Kunden, der sehr präzise Vorstellungen von dem Gebäude hatte, waren klar formuliert. Einerseits sollte sich das Museum in die Umgebung integrieren, in den vormals privaten Park rund um die herrliche Villa Berower, ein historisches Denkmal im Schweizer Ort Riehen, andererseits sollten die Säle mit Oberlicht beleuchtet werden. Um beiden Bedingungen gerecht zu werden, besteht das Projekt aus vier tragenden Mauern gleicher Länge, die parallel zu den Grenzmauern des Grundstücks verlaufen. Alle Mauern wurden mit argentinischem Sandstein verkleidet, der dem heimischen Stein ähnelt, jedoch witterungsbeständiger ist. Der gesamte Komplex wird von einem leicht geneigten Glasdach überdeckt, das dank der schwerelos wirkenden und von Innen kaum wahrnehmbaren Metallkonstruktion über dem Gebäude zu schweben scheint. Einige der Fassaden sind aus Glas, so dass die Beziehung zwischen Innen und Außen sehr intensiv ist und die Ausstellungssäle die Ruhe der Umgebung reflektieren.

Il collezionista d'arte Ernst Beyeler incaricò a Renzo Piano la costruzione di un museo che ospitasse la sua collezione. I requisiti proposti dal cliente, che possedeva una visione estremamente chiara di come doveva essere l'opera, furono sintetici. Da un lato il museo doveva essere integrato nel paesaggio: il parco, anticamente privato, che circonda la magnifica Villa Berower, un monumento storico nella località svizzera di Riehen. D'altro lato le sale dovevano essere illuminate con luce zenitale. Partendo da queste due premesse, il progetto è costituito da quattro muri portanti di uguale lunghezza, disposti parallelamente alla parete che circonda il terreno. Tutti i muri sono stati coperti con pietra arenaria dell'Argentina, che ricorda la pietra autoctona ma è più resistente alle inclemenze del tempo. Tutto il complesso è coperto da un tetto di vetro leggermente inclinato che sembra galleggiare sull'edificio grazie ad una struttura metallica leggera e quasi impercettibile dall'interno. Alcune delle facciate sono in vetro, così che la relazione tra interno ed esterno è molto intensa e le sale d'esposizione godono della calma che regna in tutta l'area.

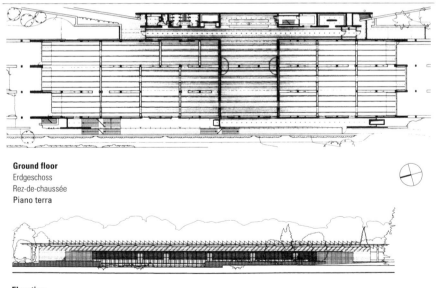

Ground floor
Erdgeschoss
Rez-de-chaussée
Piano terra

Elevation
Aufriss
Élévation
Prospetto

0   5   10

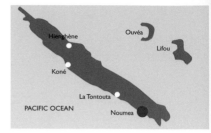

Jean Marie Tjibaou Cultural Center

Location:Beach 1000, Noumea, New Caledonia, South Pacific
Date of construction: 1991–1998
Photographers: John Gollings, Pierre Alain Pantz, William Vassal, Michel Denancé

The government of New Caledonia commissioned Renzo Piano's firm to build a cultural center in memory of the murdered Kanak leader Jean Marie Tjibaou. One of the project's basic aims was to make the building's functional requirements compatible with its role as a symbol of Kanak civilization, without falling back on merely folkloric imitations of the local architecture. The difficult task of reinterpreting Kanak huts resulted in buildings with a double shell supported by wooden ribs and beams clad with a layer of Iroko wood, echoing the intertwined vegetal fibers of the local houses. The complex, which is situated in the heart of a park surrounded by the sea and lagoons, comprises ten of these buildings, ranging from 20 to 28 meters in height and interconnected by footpaths. The various cultural activities are spread over different buildings: conference rooms, a library, temporary and permanent exhibitions, offices and a large auditorium for concerts and dance performances. In short, this project represents the realization of a painstaking effort to strike the right balance between tradition and technology.

Le gouvernement de Nouvelle Calédonie chargea l'étude de Renzo Piano de construire un centre culturel en la mémoire du leader kanak assassiné, Jean Marie Tjibaou. L'un des objectifs fondamentaux du projet était de rendre compatible le programme fonctionnel avec l'idée de construction symbolisant la civilisation kanak, tout en se différenciant d'une simple imitation folklorique de l'architecture locale. Avec pour tâche difficile de réinterpréter les huttes kanaks, des structures furent érigées, composées d'une double carapace construite à partir de nervures et de poutres de bois revêtues d'une peau en bois d'iroko, faisant référence aux fibres tissées de la végétation et des demeures locales. L'ensemble comporte dix de ces structures, de 20 à 28 mètres de haut, connectées par des allées piétonnières situées au cœur d'un parc entouré par la mer et les lagunes. Le programme se répartit entre les diverses constructions : salles de conférence, bibliothèque, expositions temporaires et permanentes, bureaux et même un grand auditorium pour les concerts et les bals. Le projet est, en définitive, la matérialisation de l'effort appliqué pour trouver le juste équilibre entre la tradition et la technologie.

Die Regierung von Neu-Kaledonien beauftragte das Studio Renzo Piano mit der Konstruktion eines Kulturzentrums in Erinnerung an den ermordeten Kanakenführer Jean Marie Tjibaou. Eine der Zielsetzungen des Projektes war, die Funktionen des Komplexes in Einklang zu bringen mit seiner Eigenschaft als Symbol der Kultur der Kanaken. Es war eine schwierige Aufgabe, die einheimische Architektur neu zu interpretieren und gleichzeitig eine folkloristische Nachahmung zu vermeiden. Konstruktionen mit Doppelstrukturen aus Holzrippen und -trägern wurden errichtet, die mit einer Haut aus Iroko-Holz verkleidet wurden, womit auf die gefärbten pflanzlichen Fasern der einheimischen Häuser angespielt werden sollte. Der Komplex besteht aus zehn dieser 20 bis 28 m hohen, durch Fußwege miteinander verbundenen Gebäude im Herzen eines von Meer und Lagunen umgebenen Parkes. Das Kulturzentrum besteht aus verschiedenen Bauten: Konferenzsäle, eine Bibliothek, Ausstellungsräume, Büros und sogar ein großes Auditorium für Konzerte und Tanzveranstaltungen. Das Projekt ist letztlich Ausdruck einer behutsamen Bemühung um das richtige Gleichgewicht zwischen Tradition und Technologie.

Il governo della Nuova Caledonia incaricò allo studio di Renzo Piano la costruzione di un centro culturale in memoria del leader kanak assassinato Jean Marie Tjibaou. Uno degli obiettivi fondamentali del progetto era rendere compatibile il programma funzionale con l'idea della costruzione come un simbolo della civiltà kanak e che inoltre si distanziasse da un'imitazione folkloristica dell'architettura locale. Nel difficile compito di reinterpretare le capanne kanak, sono state erette delle costruzioni composte da un doppio guscio, costruite con "costole" e travi in legno, rivestite da una pelle di legno di iroko, che fa allusione alle fibre intrecciate della vegetazione e delle case locali. Il complesso è composto da dieci edifici, tra 20 e 28 metri d'altezza, collegati da percorsi pedonali ubicati nel cuore di un parco circondato da mare e lagune. Il programma si divide in diverse costruzioni: sale conferenze, una biblioteca, mostre temporanee e permanenti, uffici, e perfino un gran auditorio per concerti e balletti. Il progetto è, in definitiva, la materializzazione dell'attento sforzo per trovare il giusto equilibrio tra tradizione e tecnologia.

Plan
Lageplan
Localisation
Piano

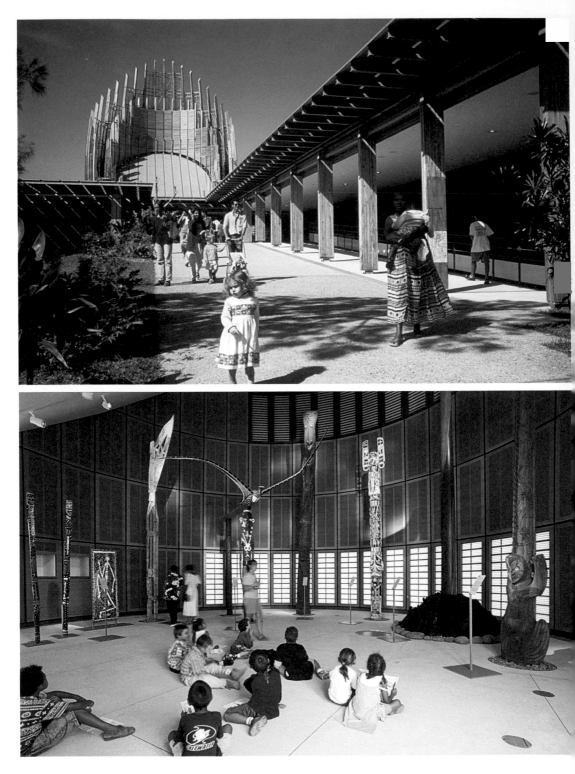

Cross section Querschnitt
Section transversale Sezione traversale

0 2 4

Reconstruction of Potsdamer Platz

Location: Potsdamer Platz, Berlin, Germany
Date of construction: 1992–2000
Photographers: Gianni Berengo Gardin, Vincent Mosch, Enrico Cano, Michel Denancé

Shortly after the reunification of Germany several competitions were held for projects designed to renovate the center of Berlin. Renzo Piano's firm was chosen to regenerate Potsdamer Platz, where only one building, the Weinhaus Huth, had remained standing after the war. The project, promoted by the Daimler-Chrysler corporation, comprises 18 buildings, connected by pedestrian streets and a square; its proportions are on a human scale, encouraging the locals to stroll in the neighborhood which is lively and also peaceful thanks to its trees and fountains. The eight buildings designed by Piano aim to create a whole that is consistent without being uniform so, although the same materials are used throughout, they are subject to a variety of treatments and finishings. The first building to be put up was B1, a 195-foot high office block with a glass façade superimposed on a terracota front. The buildings B3 and B10 contain commercial premises and B5 is a residential block with an inner garden. The other buildings house a cinema (B7), offices for Débis (C1), a subsidiary of the development company, a theater and a casino (D1-D2).

Kurz nach der Wiedervereinigung Deutschlands wurden mehrere Wettbewerbe für die Renovierung des Stadtkerns von Berlin ausgeschrieben. Das Büro von Renzo Piano wurde mit der Neugestaltung des Potsdamer Platzes beauftragt, auf dem nach dem Zweiten Weltkrieg nur noch das Weinhaus Huth stehen geblieben war. Das Projekt wurde von der Firma Daimler-Chrysler unterstützt und umfasst 18, durch Fußgängerwege miteinander verbundene Gebäude, des Weiteren einen Platz, der die Stadtbewohner zum Bummeln in diesem geschäftigen Stadtteil einlädt, der jedoch dank der Bäume und Brunnen auch Ruhe ausstrahlt. Die acht von Piano entworfenen Gebäude bilden einen zusammenhängenden, jedoch keineswegs eintönigen Komplex, bei dem zwar gleiche, aber unterschiedlich behandelte Materialien mit verschieden gestalteten Oberflächen zum Einsatz kamen. Das erste fertiggestellte Gebäude ist der 60 m hohe Büroturm B1, bei dem auf den Terrakotta-Untergrund eine Glasfassade angebracht wurde. In den Gebäuden B3 und B10 befinden sich Geschäfte und B5 ist ein Wohnblock mit einem Innengarten. In anderen Gebäuden sind ein Kino (B7), die Büroräume von Débis (C1), eine Zweigstelle der Baufirma, ein Theater und ein Casino (D1-D2) untergebracht.

Peu après la réunification allemande, plusieurs concours furent organisés afin de rénover le centre de Berlin. Le cabinet de Renzo Piano fut sélectionné pour régénérer la Potsdamer Platz, où seule une construction, le Weinhaus Huth, restait debout après la guerre. Le projet, soutenu par l'entreprise Daimler-Chrysler, comporte 18 bâtiments connectés par des rues piétonnières et une place à échelle humaine qui incite les citoyens à la flânerie dans un quartier actif auquel arbres et fontaines apportent cependant une certaine tranquillité. Les huit édifices conçus par l'étude de Piano tendent à créer un ensemble cohérent sans être uniforme. De ce fait, si les mêmes matériaux ont pu être utilisés pour chacun d'eux, leur traitement et leur finition se sont révélés différents. Le premier bâtiment construit fut le B1, une tour de bureaux de 60 mètres de haut avec une façade en verre superposée sur une enveloppe en terre cuite. Les bâtiments B3 et B10 abritent des espaces commerciaux et le B5 est un bloc de logements avec jardin intérieur. De même ont été levées des constructions pour un cinéma (B7), les bureaux de Débis (C1), une filiale du promoteur, un théâtre et un casino (D1-D2).

Poco dopo l'unificazione tedesca furono convocati diversi concorsi per ristrutturare il centro di Berlino. Lo studio di Renzo Piano fu quello scelto per rinnovare la Postdamer Platz, dove dopo la guerra era rimasta un'unica costruzione intatta, lo Weinhaus Huth. Il progetto, promosso dalla ditta Daimler-Chrysler, è composto da 18 edifici, collegati da strade pedonali e da una piazza a scala d'uomo che invita i cittadini a passeggiare per la zona, piena di attività ma anche di alberi e fontane che le conferiscono tranquillità. Gli otto edifici che progettò lo studio di Piano cercano di dare forma a un insieme solidale anche se non uniforme, per cui anche se sono stati utilizzati gli stessi materiali vi sono stati applicati diversi trattamenti e finiture. Il primo edificio costruito fu il B1, un grattacielo per uffici di 60 metri d'altezza con una facciata di vetro sovrapposta a una chiusura di terracotta. Gli edifici B3 e B10 ospitano spazi commerciali ed il B5 è un condominio con un giardino interno. Sono stati inoltre costruiti edifici per un cinema (B7), gli uffici della Débis (C1), ditta sussidiaria della promotrice, un teatro ed un casinò (D1 – D2).

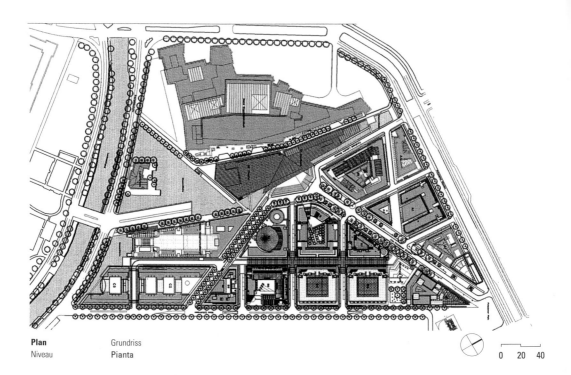

Plan
Niveau

Grundriss
Pianta

0 20 40

Elevation
Élévation

Aufriss
Prospetto

0 10 20

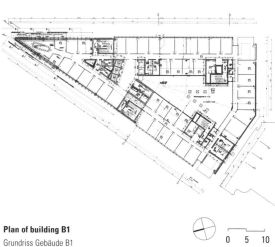

Plan of building B1
Grundriss Gebäude B1
Niveau du bâtiment B1
Pianta dell'edificio B1

0   5   10

Elevation of Marlene-Dietrich-Platz
Aufriss Marlene-Dietrich-Platz
Élévation de la Marlene-Dietrich-Platz
Prospetto della Marlene-Dietrich-Platz

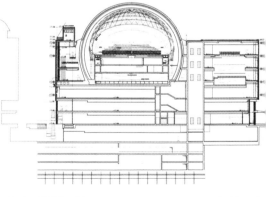

Section of building B7
Schnitt Gebäude B7
Section du bâtiment B7
Sezioni dell'edificio B7

0   3   6

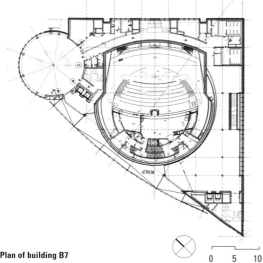

Plan of building B7
Grundriss Gebäude B7
Niveau du bâtiment B7
Pianta dell'edificio B7

0   5   10

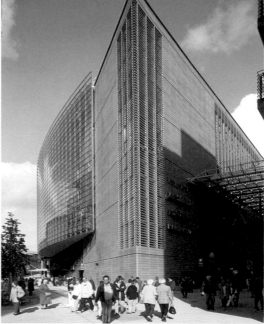

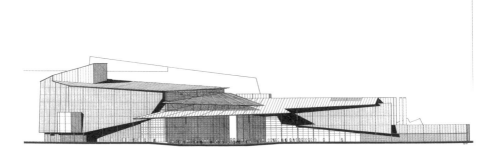

Elevation of building D1-D2
Aufriss Gebäude D1-D2
Élévation du bâtiment D1-D2
Prospetto dell'edificio D1-D2

0   8   16

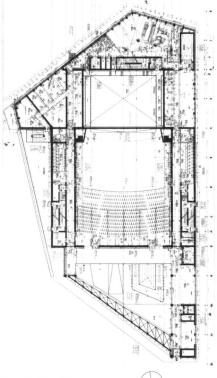

Plan of building D2
Grundriss Gebäude D2
Niveau du bâtiment D2
Pianta dell'edificio D2

0   3   6

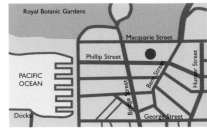

Aurora Place

Location: 88 Phillip Street, Sydney, Australia
Date of construction: 1996–2000
Photographer: John Gollings, Olaf De Nooyer, Martin van der Wal

In order to celebrate the 2000 Olympic Games the Australian Lend Lease Development company commissioned the design and construction of Aurora Place, comprising an office block and a multi-residential building in Sydney's historic center. The fact that the site was located close to the emblematic Opera House demanded a high degree of formal sensitivity in the design process. The project's two buildings are connected by a square covered by a glass roof. The 44-floor skyscraper containing the offices seems to resemble the sail of a boat that unfurls as it gains height. In order to create a relationship between the different stories, large courtyards with gardens were put in, providing light and ventilation. The glass panels that clad most of the structure emphasize the purity of the lines. This glass casing, wrapping the building as if it were its skin, extends over the whole complex to bestow transparency, dynamism and lightness. Piano has created a huge building of monumental proportions that nevertheless exudes humanity and proves comfortable and welcoming.

Pour célébrer les Jeux Olympiques de l'an 2000, l'entreprise australienne Lend Lease Development commanda la création et la construction d'une tour de bureaux et d'un bâtiment multirésidentiel baptisés Aurora Place, dans le centre historique de Sydney. L'emplacement particulier du terrain, proche de l'édifice emblématique de l'Opéra, imposait une sensibilité formelle prononcée lors de la conception. Le projet comporte deux bâtiments connectés par une place couverte d'un porche vitré. Le gratte-ciel de bureaux affiche 44 étages et ressemble, à première vue, à la voile d'un bateau se déployant à mesure qu'elle s'élève. Afin de mettre en relation les différents niveaux, de vastes patios paysagers ont eté introduits, offrant lumière et ventilation naturelles. Les panneaux de verre revêtant une grande partie de la structure soulignent à l'extrême la pureté des lignes. Cette enveloppe de verre, la véritable peau de l'édifice, s'étend sur tout l'ensemble et lui apporte transparence, dynamisme et légèreté. Avec Aurora Place, Piano arrive à ériger une construction immense, monumentale mais pour autant rayonnant d'humanité tout en demeurant confortable et accueillante.

Anlässlich der Olympischen Spiele 2000 beauftragte die australische Firma Lend Lease Development Entwurf und Konstruktion eines Büroturmes und eines Wohngebäudes mit dem Namen Aurora Place im historischen Stadtzentrum von Sydney. Die besondere Lage des Grundstückes in der Nähe des anspruchsvollen Opernhauses erforderte große formale Sensibilität bei der Ausarbeitung des Entwurfes. Das Projekt umfasst zwei Gebäude, die über einen mit Glas überdachten Platz miteinander verbunden sind. Der 44-stöckige Wolkenkratzer der Büros gleicht dem Segel eines Bootes, das sich bei zunehmender Höhe immer weiter entfaltet. Für die Verbindung der verschiedenen Etagen wurden große, bepflanzte Höfe angelegt, die für Licht und Lüftung sorgen. Die Glaspaneele, die einen großen Teil der Konstruktion bedecken, betonen die Reinheit der Linien. Dieser Glasmantel, die eigentliche Haut des Gebäudes, bedeckt es und verleiht ihm Transparenz, Dynamik und Leichtigkeit. Mit Aurora Place errichtet Piano ein gewaltiges, monumentales Gebäude, das jedoch gleichzeitig Menschlichkeit ausstrahlt und Komfort und Gemütlichkeit bietet.

Per celebrare i Giochi Olimpici del 2000, l'impresa australiana Lend Lease Development incaricò il progetto e la costruzione di un grattacielo per uffici e di un edificio residenziale chiamato Aurora Place, nel centro storico di Sidney. La particolare ubicazione del terreno, vicino all'emblematico edificio dell'opera, richiedeva una marcata sensibilità formale nel processo di progettazione. Il progetto è composto da due costruzioni collegate da una piazza, coperta con un portico vetrato. Il grattacielo degli uffici ha 44 piani e a colpo d'occhio assomiglia alla vela di una nave che si spiega all'aumentare in altezza. Per mettere in relazione i diversi piani sono stati introdotti dei grandi giardini interni che offrono luce e ventilazione naturale. I pannelli di vetro che rivestono gran parte della struttura sottolineano straordinariamente la purezza delle linee. Questo involucro di vetro, la pelle dell'edificio, si espande lungo il complesso e gli concede trasparenza, dinamicità e leggerezza. Con l'Aurora Place, Piano riesce a costruire un edificio immenso, monumentale, però che allo stesso tempo esala umanità e risulta confortevole e accogliente.

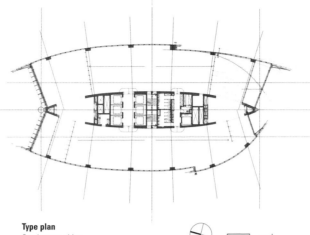

Type plan
Geschossgrundriss
Étage type
Pianta tipo

0   8   16

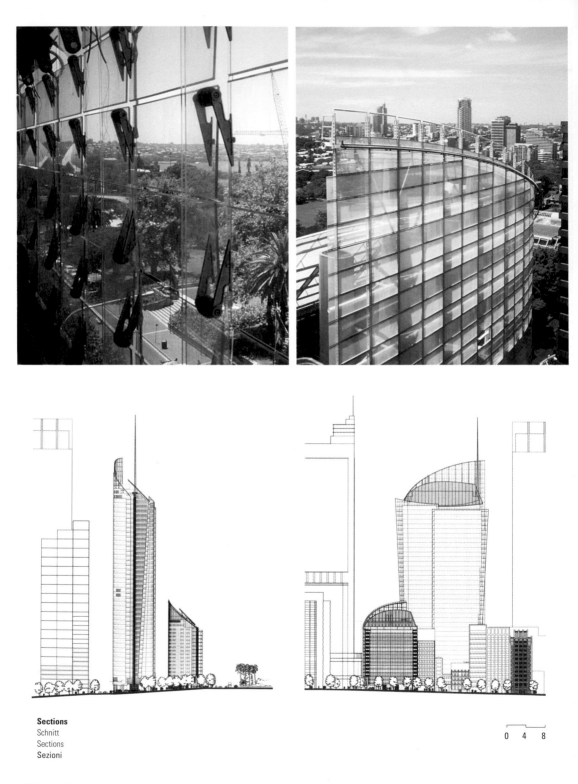

Sections
Schnitt
Sections
Sezioni

0 4 8

Niccolò Paganini Auditorium

Location: Viale Barilla, Parma, Italy
Date of construction: 1997–2001
Photographer: Enrico Cano

The Niccolò Paganini Auditorium was built inside the old Eridania sugar factory, an industrial complex made up of several buildings in a variety of styles. These manufacturing premises are located near Parma's historic center, in a park studded with indigenous trees and shrubs. The factory's conversion into an auditorium was made possible by the original layout – which enabled all the installations to be fitted in with ease – as well as its privileged position in the middle of the park, which made it easier to soundproof the auditorium. The original façades were replaced by large glass walls, which endow the entire building with light and views – wonderful views of the surroundings can even be enjoyed from the seats inside the hall. A series of panels covered with acoustic insulating material suspended from the beams provides the finishing touches to the interior spatial organization. The audience enters the complex from the southernmost point and crosses a covered courtyard to arrive at the double-height foyer that leads on to the large concert hall. The 2,700-square foot stage to the north can hold big orchestras and choirs.

Das Niccolò Paganini Auditorium wurde in den Innenräumen der alten Zuckerfabrik Eridania gebaut, einem Industriegebiet mit mehreren verschiedenen Gebäuden. Der Fabrikkomplex liegt in der Nähe des historischen Stadtzentrums von Parma inmitten eines Parks mit einheimischen Bäumen und Büschen. Der Umbau der Fabrik in einen Konzertsaal konnte dank der ursprünglichen Dimensionen des Gebäudes verwirklicht werden, die den bequemen Einbau aller Anlagen erlaubten. Dank der bevorzugten Lage des Grundstückes inmitten des Parkes wurde die Isolierung des Auditoriums vereinfacht. Große Glaswände ersetzen die vorhandenen Fassaden, gewähren den Einfall von Licht und bieten selbst von den Sitzen der Halle aus großartige Ausblicke auf die Umgebung. Ein an Trägern abgehängtes Paneelsystem mit akustischer Isolierung vervollständigt die räumliche Anordnung der Innenausstattung. Der Eingang für das Publikum liegt im Süden des Gebäudes und führt nach Überqueren eines überdeckten Hofes in die sehr hohe Eingangshalle zum großen Konzertsaal. Die Bühne im Norden mit einer Fläche von 250 m² stellt genügend Platz für große Orchester und Chöre zur Verfügung.

L'auditorium Niccolò Paganini fut construit à l'intérieur de l'ancienne usine sucrière Eridania, un complexe industriel formé de différents édifices de natures diverses. L'ensemble industriel se situe près du centre historique de Parme, dans un parc peuplé d'arbres et d'arbustes autochtones. La conversion de l'usine en auditorium fut possible de par les dimensions originales des constructions permettant de placer aisément toutes les installations des équipements, mais aussi grâce à la situation particulière du terrain au cœur du parc, simplifiant les impératifs d'insonorisation de l'auditorium. Aux façades existantes furent substituées de grandes parois de verre offrant lumière et vues à tout l'édifice. Même depuis les sièges de la salle il est possible de bénéficier de vues magnifiques alentours. Un système de panneaux couverts d'isolant acoustique, suspendus aux poutres, complète l'organisation spatiale intérieure. Le public entre par l'extrême sud de l'édifice et, après avoir traversé un patio couvert, accède au hall d'entrée à double hauteur qui mène à la grande salle de concerts. La scène, située au nord et affichant quelque 250 m² de superficie peut accueillir les grands orchestres et les chœurs.

L'auditorio Niccolò Paganini è stato costruito all'interno dell'antica fabbrica di zucchero Eridania, un impianto manifatturiero formato da varie costruzioni. Il complesso industriale è situato vicino al centro storico di Parma, in un parco popolato di alberi ed arbusti autoctoni. La trasformazione della fabbrica in auditorio è stata possibile grazie alle dimensioni originarie delle strutture che hanno permesso di collocare comodamente tutti gli impianti, ed anche alla particolare situazione del lotto, situato in mezzo al parco, che ha semplificato l'insonorizzazione dell'auditorio. Le facciate esistenti sono state sostituite da grandi pareti vetrate che assicurano luce e vedute a tutto l'edificio: perfino dalle poltrone della sala si possono gustare i magnifici panorami dell'intorno. Un sistema di pannelli coperti da isolante acustico, appesi alle travi, completa l'organizzazione spaziale degli interni. Il pubblico entra dall'estremità sud della costruzione e, dopo aver attraversato un giardino coperto, accede all'atrio a doppia altezza che porta alla grande sala concerti. Lo scenario, situato a nord e con 250 m². di superficie, può accogliere grandi orchestre e cori.

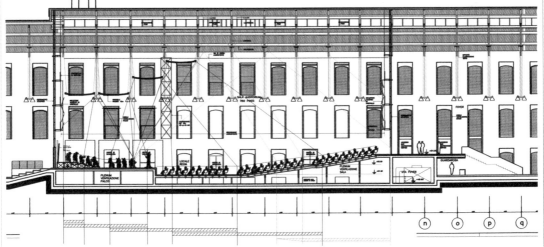

Longitudinal section
Längsschnitt
Section longitudinale
Sezione longitudinale

0 2 4

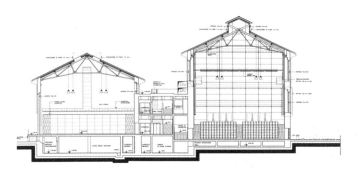

Cross section
Section transversale

Querschnitt
Sezione trasversale

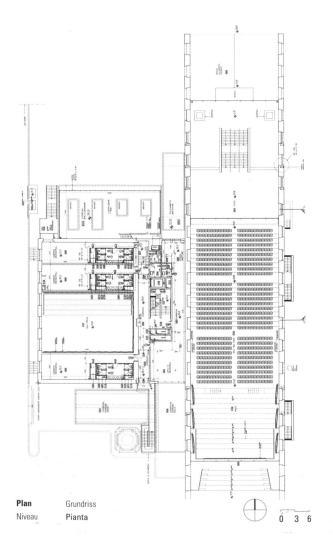

Plan
Niveau

Grundriss
Pianta

0 3 6

Maison Hermès

Location: 4-3 Ginza 5 Chome, Chuo-ku, Tokyo, Japan
Date of construction: 1998-2001
Photographers: Michel Denancé

The French Hermès group chose Tokyo's central Ginza district as the site for its Japanese headquarters, which comprise commercial outlets, workshops, offices and showrooms spread over 64,500 square feet and crowned by a French-style roof garden. The project represented an aesthetic and technical challenge as it had to blend into the urban setting around it while also guaranteeing stability in the face of possible earthquakes. The building's façades, spanning fifteen floors and a rectangular perimeter, are entirely made up of prefabricated glass blocks measuring 9 x 9 inches. These elements were specially designed and built for the project, in order to form a luminous and uninterrupted barrier between the peacefulness of the interior and the hubbub of the city, as well as providing a traditional yet technological touch. In order to prevent any damage in the event of an earthquake, an innovative structural system was designed; this consists of a flexible steel truss, articulated at strategic points by buffers that absorb any possible movements made by the structure and also strengthen the building's floors.

Le groupe français Hermès choisit le district central de Ginza pour son siège social au Japon, comptant espaces commerciaux, ateliers, bureaux et salles d'expositions répartis sur 6 000 m² et couronnés par un vaste jardin à la française. Le projet posait un défi esthétique et technique : entrer en harmonie avec l'environnement urbain qui l'accueillait tout en assurant la stabilité face à des séismes potentiels. Les façades de l'édifice, qui comporte quinze étages et un périmètre rectangulaire, sont entièrement formées de blocs de verre préfabriqués de 45 x 45 cm. Ces éléments, spécialement conçus et construits pour l'œuvre, constituent une fermeture continue et lumineuse entre la tranquillité de l'intérieur et le tohu-bohu de la ville. Ils confèrent, en outre, un air traditionnel et à la fois technologique à l'édifice. Afin de prévenir les dommages en cas de tremblement de terre, un système structurel novateur a été conçu, composé d'un cadre flexible d'acier articulé en des points stratégiques par des amortisseurs absorbant les possibles mouvements de la structure et soutenant, par surcroît, les forgeages de la construction.

Die französische Hermès Gruppe wählte diese zentrale Lage in Ginza für den Sitz ihrer Firma in Japan: Geschäftsräume, Werkstätten, Büros und Ausstellungsflächen auf 6.000 m² verteilt und gekrönt von einem großen Dachgarten im französischen Stil. Das Projekt bedeutete eine ästhetische und technische Herausforderung, denn es sollte einerseits mit seiner städtischen Umgebung harmonieren und andererseits möglichen Erdbeben standhalten. Alle Fassaden des fünfzehnstöckigen, rechteckigen Gebäudes bestehen aus vorgefertigten Glasblöcken von 45 x 45 cm. Diese eigens für diesen Bau entworfenen und hergestellten Elemente bilden eine kontinuierliche und lichtdurchlässige Trennung zwischen der Ruhe in den Innenräumen und dem Lärm der Stadt und verleihen dem Gebäude ein gleichzeitig traditionelles und technologisches Flair. Um Schäden durch eventuelle Erdbeben zu verhüten, wurde ein neues Konstruktionssystem eingesetzt, das an den strategischen Punkten Puffer aus flexiblen Stahlträgern vorsieht, die mögliche Bewegungen der Konstruktion absorbieren und außerdem den Verbund des Gebäudes stützen.

Il gruppo francese Hermès scelse il distretto centrale di Ginza per situarvi la sede della propria ditta in Giappone, che è composta da spazi commerciali, laboratori, uffici e sale mostre, distribuiti su 6.000 m² di superficie, coronati da un grande giardino in stile francese sulla copertura. Il progetto rappresentava una sfida estetica e tecnica, visto che doveva armonizzarsi con l'intorno urbano nel quale si inseriva e allo stesso tempo garantire stabilità nel caso di possibili terremoti. Le facciate dell'edificio, che ha quindici piani ed un perimetro rettangolare, sono interamente formate da blocchi prefabbricati di vetro di 45 x 45 cm. Questi elementi, appositamente realizzati per l'intervento, creano una separazione continua e luminosa tra la tranquillità dell'interno e l'animazione della città, e conferiscono inoltre un'aria tradizionale e insieme tecnologica alla costruzione. Per prevenire danni in caso di terremoti, è stato progettato un sistema strutturale innovativo, composto da un'armatura flessibile in acciaio, articolata in punti strategici da ammortizzatori che assorbono i possibili movimenti della struttura e per di più sostengono i solai della costruzione.

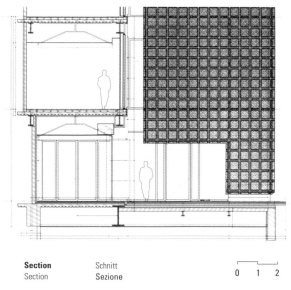

Section
Section
Schnitt
Sezione

0   1   2

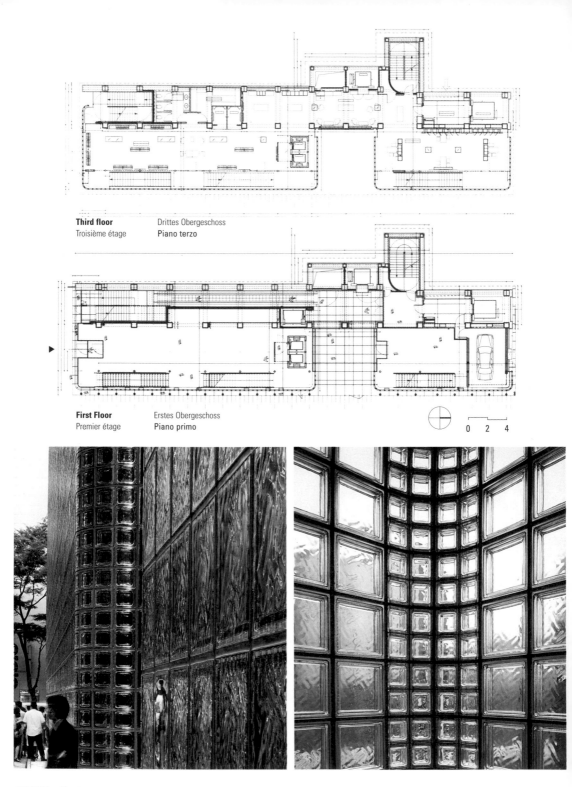

Third floor   Drittes Obergeschoss
Troisième étage   **Piano terzo**

First Floor   Erstes Obergeschoss
Premier étage   **Piano primo**

0   2   4

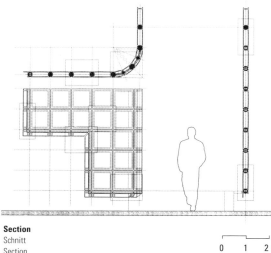

Section
Schnitt
Section
Sezione

0   1   2

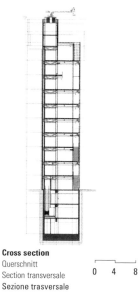

Cross section
Querschnitt
Section transversale
Sezione trasversale

0   4   8

La Bolla

Location: Palazzina San Giobatta Genoa Port, Genoa, Italy
Date of construction: 2000–2001
Photographers: Gianni Berengo Gardin, Stefano Goldberg

The team headed by Renzo Piano was commissioned to design this striking bubble-shape building for the G8 summit meeting that was held in Genoa in 2001. The project also forms part of the scheme that is underway to modernize the city's old port. A big glass ball occupies one of the quays, whose structure had to be reinforced to support the weight; it is approached via a drawbridge. Inside, visitors walk on a loosely-fitted flooring swathed in enormous tropical ferns. The casing is made of double curved glass panels, attached to the structure by supports that pass through the intersections of the panels to ensure the building's stability. The joints are sealed with elastic silicone to absorb any possible vibrations. The metal shell is made up of a series of metal tubes placed both vertically and horizontally and held together by steel clamps. The idea was to make a structure that was easy to transport; it was built in a workshop and did not require a single piece to be soldered on the construction site.

Das von Renzo Piano geleitete Team wurde anlässlich des Gipfeltreffens der G8-Staaten in Genua im Jahre 2001 mit dem Entwurf dieses eigenartigen Gebäudes in Form einer Luftblase beauftragt. Das Projekt ist ein Teil des Programmes für die Modernisierung des alten Hafens der Stadt. Auf einem der Dämme steht eine große Kristallkugel, deren Konstruktion verstärkt wurde und die über eine Zugbrücke zugänglich ist. Im Inneren geht man über einen schwingenden Boden, der von riesigen tropischen Farnen eingefasst ist. Die Ummantelung besteht aus gebogenen Doppelglaspaneelen, die über Stützbalken an der Konstruktion befestigt sind. Sie durchqueren die Platten an ihren Schnittstellen, um so die Stabilität der Konstruktion zu gewährleisten. Die Stöße sind mit elastischem Silikon abgedichtet, um eventuelle Vibrationen zu absorbieren. Das Gestell besteht aus einem System vertikaler und horizontaler Rohre, die mit Stahlflanschen verspannt sind. In der Werkstatt sollte eine leicht zu transportierende Konstruktion gebaut werden, um das Schweißen von Teilen auf der Baustelle zu vermeiden.

L'équipe dirigée par Renzo Piano fut chargée de concevoir cet édifice singulier en forme de bulle, dans l'optique de la réunion du G8 qui se tint à Gênes en 2001. Le projet forme également partie des interventions menées à bien pour moderniser l'ancien port de la ville. Une grande boule de cristal occupe l'un des quais dont il fallut renforcer la structure pour supporter la création, accessible grâce à un pont-levis. À l'intérieur, l'usager chemine sur un sol flottant entouré d'immenses fougères tropicales. L'enveloppe est formée de panneaux de verre courbés doubles, fixés à une structure à l'aide de piliers traversant les plaques en leurs intersections et assurant ainsi la stabilité de la structure. Les jointures sont scellées à l'aide de silicone élastique afin d'absorber les vibrations possibles. L'armature métallique est composée d'un système de tubes métalliques placés verticalement et horizontalement, et maintenus à l'aide de brides d'acier. La structure fut pensée pour être facile à transporter, car construite en atelier, et elle ne requit aucune soudure sur le chantier.

L'equipe guidata da Renzo Piano fu incaricata di progettare questo peculiare edificio a forma di sfera in occasione del vertice dei G8 che si è svolto a Genova nel 2001. Il progetto forma parte anche delle operazioni che si stanno portando a termine per modernizzare l'antico porto della città. Una grande sfera di cristallo occupa uno dei moli, che è stato rinforzato strutturalmente per sostenere il congegno, al quale si accede attraverso un ponte levatoio. All'interno, l'utente cammina su un pavimento galleggiante, circondato da enormi felci tropicali. Il rivestimento è formato da doppi pannelli di cristallo curvato, fissati ad una struttura mediante dei puntelli che attraversano le lastre nelle loro intersezioni, garantendo la stabilità della struttura. Le giunte sono sigillate con silicone elastico per assorbire le possibili vibrazioni. L'armatura metallica è composta da un sistema di tubi metallici collocati in senso orizzontale e verticale, e distanziati con delle flange d'acciaio. E stata ideata una struttura facile da trasportare: è stata costruita in officina e non è stato necessario saldare nessun pezzo in opera.

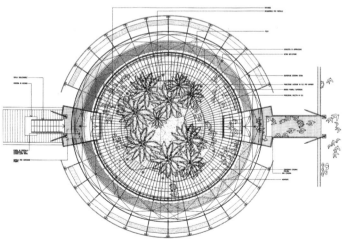

Plan
Grundriss
Niveau
Pianta

0   4   8

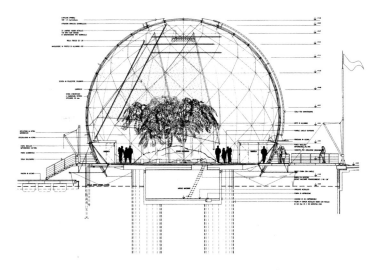

Section
Schnitt
Section
Sezione

0　2　4

Parco della Mùsica Auditorium

Location: Viale de Cobertin 14, Rome, Italy
Date of construction: 1994–2002
Photographer: Gianni Berengo Gardin, Moreno Maggi

This superb auditorium is a further addition to the Italian capital's already long list of cultural venues. It is a multipurpose center intensively devoted to music, with three concert halls surrounded by dense vegetation and laid out in such a way that they create an amphitheater for open-air performances. Each auditorium was planned to put on a certain type of performance. So, the 700-seater is intended for Baroque and chamber music; the 1,200-seater is characterized by its great flexibility, enabling it to accommodate large orchestras and ballets, while the largest, with 2,800 seats – the maximum capacity guaranteeing good acoustics – is designed for symphonic concerts. The project placed a special emphasis on the acoustics in all the spaces, including the rehearsal rooms, the dressing rooms and the amphitheater. Flexibility was another top priority in the brief as the complex had to be able to absorb different groups of spectators. The remains of a villa dating from the fourth century BC were found during the building works, and so the main foyer had to be adapted to this site and make room for a small archeological museum.

L'auditorium flambant neuf de la capitale italienne vient s'ajouter à la longue liste d'équipements culturels de la ville, avec un centre multifonctionnel dédié exclusivement à la musique. Les trois salles de concert réalisées sont entourées d'une végétation dense et s'organisent sur le terrain en générant un amphithéâtre pour les spectacles à l'air libre. Chaque auditorium a été projeté pour s'offrir à un type de spectacle déterminé. Ainsi, celui de 700 places a été pensé pour la musique de chambre et baroque; celui de 1 200 places se caractérise par une plus grande flexibilité afin de pouvoir accueillir de grands orchestres et des ballets : enfin la salle dotée de 2 800 sièges, la capacité maximale pour une acoustique optimale, a été conçue pour les concerts symphoniques. Le développement du projet a donné la priorité à l'acoustique dans tous les lieux du complexe, même pour les salles de répétition, les halls et l'amphithéâtre. La flexibilité également était l'un des imposés de la commande, diverses affluences de spectateurs devant pouvoir être absorbées. Lors des travaux, les restes d'une villa du IVème siècle av. J.C. furent mis à jour. De ce fait, le hall principal dut s'adapter à la découverte et héberger un petit musée archéologique.

Dieses aufsehenerregende Auditorium kann als multifunktionelles, ausschließlich der Musik geweihtes Zentrum der ohnehin schon langen Liste kultureller Einrichtungen in Rom hinzugefügt werden. Die drei Konzertsäle, von dichter Vegetation umsäumt, sind so angelegt, dass sie als Amphitheater für Aufführungen im Freien eingesetzt werden können. Jedes Auditorium wurde für eine bestimmte Art Musik entworfen. So ist z.B. der Saal mit 700 Sitzplätzen für Kammer- und Barockmusik gedacht; der Saal mit 1200 Plätzen ist ausgesprochen flexibel, so dass große Orchester sowie Ballette hier Platz finden; der große Saal mit 2800 Plätzen, die oberste Grenze für eine gute Akustik, wurde Symphoniekonzerten vorbehalten. Während der Entwicklung des Projektes wurde in allen Räumen des Komplexes, einschließlich der Probesäle, der Eingangshallen und des Amphitheaters großen Wert auf die Akustik gelegt. Flexibilität bezüglich der Aufnahmekapazität gehörte aufgrund des Besucherandrangs ebenfalls zu den Bedingungen des Auftrags. Während der Arbeiten wurden die Ruinen eines Hauses aus dem 4. Jahrhundert a.C. gefunden, die heute in einem kleinen archäologischen Museum im Haupteingang zu besichtigen sind, welcher den neuen Gegebenheiten angepasst werden musste.

Il fiammante auditorio della capitale italiana somma alla lunga lista di attrezzature culturali della città un centro multifunzionale dedicato interamente alla musica. Le tre sale per concerti costruite sono circondate da una densa vegetazione e sono state distribuite sul terreno in modo da creare ad un anfiteatro per spettacoli all'aria aperta. Ogni auditorio è stato progettato per accogliere una determinata varietà di spettacoli. Così che quello da 700 posti è stato pensato per la musica da camera e barocca; quello da 1200 posti è caratterizzato da una gran flessibilità per poter accogliere sia grandi orchestre che balletti; e quello da 2800 posti, la massima capacità di una sala per garantire una buona acustica, è stato progettato per concerti sinfonici. L'elaborazione del progetto ha dato la priorità all'acustica in tutti i locali del complesso, incluse le sale per le prove, gli ingressi e l'anfiteatro. Anche la flessibilità era uno dei requisiti dell'incarico, visto che era necessario poter assorbire differenti affluenze di spettatori. Durante le opere si scoprirono i resti di una villa del IV° secolo. a.C. così che il vestibolo principale dovette adattarsi per ospitare un piccolo museo.

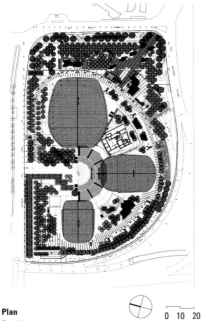

Plan
Grundriss
Niveau
Pianta

0 10 20

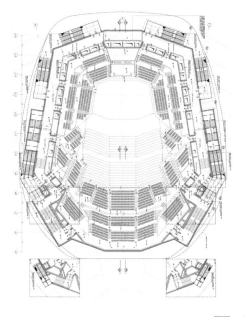

Plan of the 2.800 seats building
Grundriss des Gebäudes mit 2.800 Plätzen
Niveau du bâtiment pour 2.800 sièges
Pianta dell'edificio da 2.800 posti

0 8 16

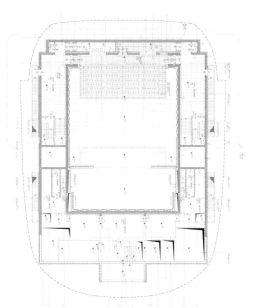

Plan of the 700 seats building
Grundriss des Gebäudes mit 700 Plätzen
Niveau du bâtiment pour 700 sièges
Pianta dell'edificio da 700 posti

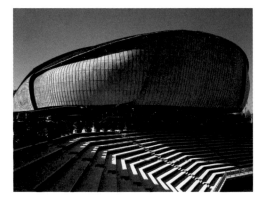

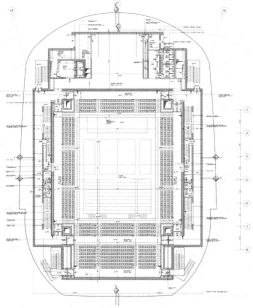

Plan of the 1.200 seats building
Grundriss des Gebäudes mit 1.200 Plätzen
Niveau du bâtiment pour 1.200 sièges
Pianta dell'edificio da 1.200 posti

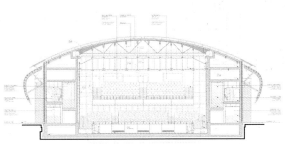

Cross section of the 700 seats building
Querschnitt des Gebäudes mit 700 Plätzen
Section transversale du bâtiment pour 700 sièges
Sezione trasversale dell'edificio da 700 posti

0 3 6

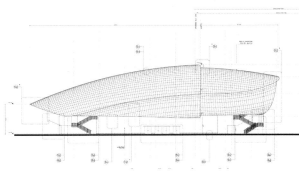

Elevation of the 1.200 seats building
Aufriss des Gebäudes mit 1.200 Plätzen
Élévation du bâtiment pour 1.200 sièges
Prospetto dell'edificio da 1.200 posti

0 2 4

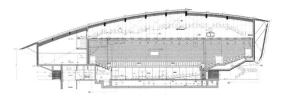

Cross section of the 1.200 seats building
Querschnitt des Gebäudes mit 1.200 Plätzen
Section transversale du bâtiment pour 1.200 sièges
Sezione trasversale dell'edificio da 1.200 posti

0 3 6

Padre Pio Church

Location: San Giovanni Rotondo, Foggia, Italy
Date of construction: 1991–2003
Photographers: Gianni Berengo Gardin, Vittorio Grassi, Michel Denancé

Since Padre Pio's death thousands of pilgrims flock to the San Giovanni Rotondo complex to pay tribute to him. The head of the Capuchin monastery that Padre Pio belonged to commissioned Renzo Piano to build a new church capable of accommodating all the worshippers that travel to the spot every year. The site, set on a hill top, has its own access road, to prevent the town from being burdened by the cars of so many visitors. A wall with twelve big bells bounds this road, and it also serves to highlight the church, which otherwise goes unnoticed among the surrounding trees. One of the project's aims was to create an open building that, despite its scale, would not overwhelm its congregation; so a light glass front was designed. This also serves to establish a relationship between the interior and the exterior, which is also emphasized by the unification of the flooring. The latest technological developments made it possible to build the entire church out of stone: the floors, the ceiling and the structural system, made up of arches spanning more than fifty meters. The use of a single material endows the setting with great expressive power.

Depuis la mort du Padre Pio, des milliers de fidèles se rendent au complexe de San Giovanni Rotondo pour lui rendre hommage. Le responsable du monastère capucin auquel appartenait le père chargea Renzo Piano de la construction d'une nouvelle église qui serait à même d'accueillir les dévots se rendant chaque année en ce lieu. Le projet, situé en haut d'une colline, dispose d'un accès indépendant afin de libérer le village des véhicules des visiteurs. Un mur présentant douze cloches limite cette route et sert de leurre pour une église passant inaperçue entre les arbres environnants. Un des principaux objectifs était de créer un lieu ouvert qui, en dépit de son ampleur, saurait ne pas intimider les visiteurs. Ainsi fut écartée la construction d'une façade monumentale pour laisser la place à une clôture de verre. De cette façon, naît une relation entre l'intérieur et l'extérieur qui est mise en exergue avec l'unification du pavage. Grâce aux nouvelles technologies, l'édifice sera monté en pierre dans sa quasi-intégralité : sols, toit et le système structurel constitué d'arcs de plus de cinquante mètres de portée. C'est le recours à un matériau unique qui confère une telle expressivité à l'ensemble.

Seit dem Tod des Paters Pio sind Tausende von Gläubigen zu den Komplex von San Giovanni Rotondo gepilgert, um ihm Ehre zu erweisen und seiner zu gedenken. Der Vorsteher des Kapuziner klosters, dem Pater Pio angehörte, beauftragte Renzo Piano mit dem Bau einer neuen Kirche zur Unterbringung der Andächtigen die jedes Jahr an diesem Ort zusammentrafen. Die Kirche erhebt sich auf einem Hügel mit eigener Zufahrt, um das Dorf vor den Fahr zeugen der Besucher zu verschonen. Eine Mauer mit zwölf große Glocken begrenzt diese Straße und lockt den Besucher zu der zwi schen Bäumen versteckten Kirche. In der Absicht, ein trotz seine Umfangs offenes, Vertrauen erweckendes Gebäude zu schaffen entschied man sich für eine Glasfront. So entstand eine Beziehun zwischen Innen und Außen, die durch das einheitliche Pflaster noc unterstrichen wird. Dank der neuen Technologien konnte praktisc das gesamte Gebäude in Stein gebaut werden: Fußböden, Dac und das strukturelle System aus Bögen mit mehr als fünfzig Meter Spannweite. Die ausschließliche Verwendung eines einzigen Mate rials verleiht dem Komplex große Ausdrucksfähigkeit.

Dalla morte di Padre Pio migliaia di fedeli affluiscono al com plesso di San Giovanni Rotondo per rendergli omaggio. I responsabile del monastero dei cappuccini al quale apparte neva Padre Pio, incaricò a Renzo Piano la costruzione di una nuova chiesa capace di ospitare i devoti che ogni anno si muo vono verso la località. Il progetto, situato in cima a una collina ha un accesso indipendente per liberare il paese dai veicoli de visitatori. Un muro con dodici grandi campane limita questa strada e serve da richiamo per una chiesa che passa inosser vata tra gli alberi dell'intorno. Uno dei principali obiettivi era creare un edificio aperto che, nonostante la sua importanza non intimidisse gli utilizzatori, per cui si scartò l'idea di eriger una facciata monumentale e si progettò una chiusura di vetro In questo modo si stabilisce una relazione tra l'interno e l'ester no che viene enfatizzata dall'unità della pavimentazione. Grazi alle nuove tecnologie, praticamente tutto l'edificio sarà realiz zato in pietra: pavimenti, tetto ed il sistema strutturale costituit da archi di più di cinquanta metri di luce. L'utilizzo di un unic materiale apporta una forte espressività all'insieme.

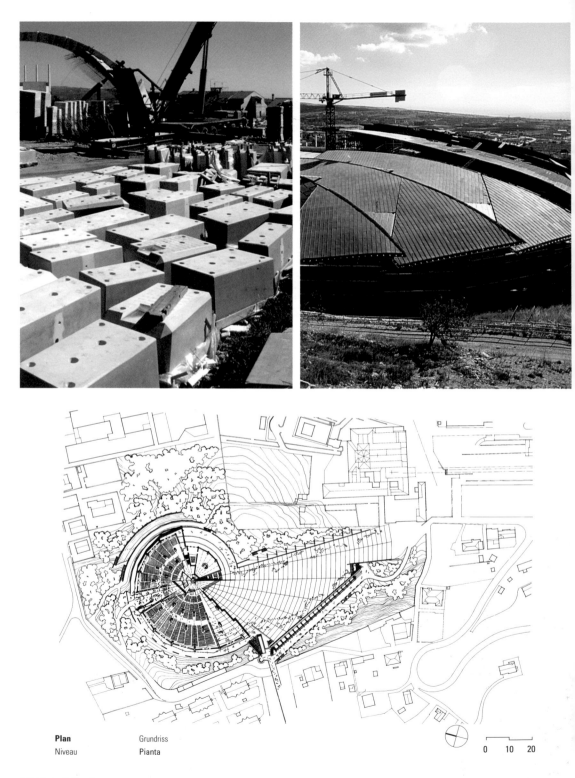

Plan   Grundriss
Niveau   Pianta

0   10   20

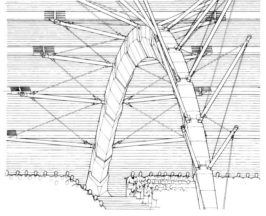

Credits

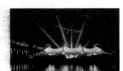

Columbus International Exhibition , Genoa, Italy
Client: City of Genoa
Consultants: Ove Arup & Partners; Italimpianti; L. Mascia/D. Mascia; P. Costa; L. Lembo; V. Nascimbene; A.Ballerini;
G. Malcangi; Sidercard; M. Testone; G. F. Visconti; Manens Intertecnica; M. Semino; Cambridge Seven Associates; F. Doria,
M. Giacomelli; S. Lanzon; B. Merello; M. Nouvion; G. Robotti; A. Savioli; STED; D. Commins; P. Castiglioni; E. Piras; L. Moni;
Scène; Cetena; G. Macchi; Origoni & Steiner

Beyeler Foundation, Riehen (Basel), Switzerland
Client: The Beyeler Foundation
Project in collaboration with: Burckhardt + Partner AG (Basel)
Consultants: Ove Arup & Partners; C. Burger + Partner AG; Bogenschütz AG; J. Forrer AG; Elektrizitäts AG; J. Wiede;
Schönholzer + Stauffer

Jean Marie Tjibaou Cultural Center, Noumea, New Caledonia
Client: Agence pour le Développement de la Culture Kanak
Consultants: A. Bensa; Desvigne & Dalnoky; Ove Arup & Partners; GEC Ingénierie; Scène; CSTB; Agibat MTI;
Peutz & Associés; Qualiconsult; Végétude; Intégral R. Baur

Reconstruction of Potsdamer Platz, Berlin, Germany
Client: Daimler-Chrysler AG
Project in association with: Christoph Kohlbecker (Gaggenau)
Consultants: Boll & Partners/Ove Arup & Partners; IBF Dr. Falkner GmbH/Weiske & Partner; IGH/Ove Arup & Partners,
Schmidt-Reuter & Partner; Müller BBM; Hundt & Partner; IBB Burrer; Ove Arup & Partners; ITF Intertraffic; Atelier Dreiseitl;
Krüger & Möhrle; P. L. Copat; Drees & Sommer/Kohlbecker

Aurora Place, Sydney, Australia
Client: Lend Lease Development
Project in collaboration with: Lend Lease Design Group (Sydney)
Consultants: Lend Lease Design Group Ltd.; Ove Arup & Partners; Taylor Thomson Whitting

Niccolò Paganini Auditorium, Parma, Italy
Client: City of Parma
Consultants: Müller BBM; P. Costa; Manens Intertecnica; Paghera; Studio Galli; Amitaf; Austin Italia; F. Santolini;
Gierrevideo

Maison Hermès, Tokyo, Japan
Client: Hermès Japon
Project in collaboration with: Rena Dumas Architecture Intérieure (Paris)
Consultants: Ove Arup & Partners; Syllabus; Delph; Ph. Almon; R. Labeyrie; K. Tanaka; Atelier 10/N. Takata; ArchiNova
Associates; Takenaka Corporation Design Department; S. Shingu

La Bolla, Genoa, Italy
Client: Porto Antico di Genova SpA
Consultants: Techint SpA; Ove Arup & Partners; Polar Glassin System; Tekne; Studio Galli S.r.l.; Mageco; P. Castiglioni;
C. Manfreddo; P. Nalin

Parco della Mùsica Auditorium, Rome, Italy
Client: City of Rome
Consultants: Studio Vitone & Associati; Manens Intertecnica; Müller-BBM; T. Gatehouse; Austin Italia; F. Zagari, E. Trabella;
Tecnocons; P. L. Cerri, Techint/Drees & Sommer

Padre Pio Church, San Giovanni Rotondo (Foggia), Italy
Client: Frati Minori Cappuccini (Province of Foggia)
Consultants: Ove Arup & Partners; Manens Intertecnica; Müller BBM; G. Muciaccia; Austin Italia; G. Amadeo; Tecnocons;
STED; Studio Ambiente; Favero & Milan; CO.RE. Ingegneria; Mons. C. Valenziano; G. Grasso o.p.